David

Clever Stuff
you can do
Online to make
and save money

In easy steps is an imprint of In Easy Steps Limited
4 Chapel Court · 42 Holly Walk · Leamington Spa
Warwickshire · United Kingdom · CV32 4YS
www.ineasysteps.com

Notice of Liability
Every effort has been made to ensure that this book contains accurate and current information. However, In Easy Steps Limited and the author shall not be liable for any loss or damage suffered by readers as a result of any information contained herein. All prices stated in the book are correct at the time of printing.

Trademarks
All trademarks are acknowledged as belonging to their respective companies.

In Easy Steps Limited supports The Forest Stewardship Council (FSC), the leading international forest certification organisation. All our titles that are printed on Greenpeace approved FSC certified paper carry the FSC logo.

MIX
Paper from
responsible sources
FSC® C020837

Printed and bound in the United Kingdom
ISBN 978-1-84078-568-5

Contents

1 Clear out your clutter

Are you a hoarder or do you just have a lot of items in your home that you do not use?

Whatever your motivation, selling online is a fast way to make money whether you sell by auction or at a price set by yourself.

Selling items online

It is often said that one man's trash is another man's treasure. That is very much true when it comes to websites such as eBay which, for years, have allowed you to quickly sell your unwanted items.

Selling items online is far more effective than selling face-to-face from a market, garage or the back of a motor. It allows you to:

- Potentially sell to a worldwide audience

- Have your items available to view 24-hours-a-day

- Set your own rates or allow buyers to bid

- Conduct sales safely and with protection

- Relax and wait for a sale, so making efficient use of your time

And there are numerous ways of selling online.

As well as eBay, which is perhaps the most well known method, you can also choose from Amazon Marketplace where your goods will appear on the world's largest retail website or you can decide to opt for the classified ad services offered by Gumtree and Craigslist.

There are many other websites too but we are going to concentrate on this selection.

Introducing eBay

The story goes that eBay began life in 1995 to allow the girlfriend of founder Pierre Omidyar to sell Pez dispensers to a wide audience. Whether or not that is true matters little. The fact is that eBay remains a brilliant way to sell unwanted items.

With eBay you can:

- Sell items at a fixed Buy It Now price

- Allow users to bid on your item

- Invite buyers to make you an offer

You can also control how your item appears online, set postage rates and communicate with buyers. The feedback scheme lets you see the reputation of the people with whom you deal.

Signing up to eBay

1. Click register on the homepage at ebay.com

2. Select your country and fill in your personal details

3. Create a user ID and password and pick a secret question

4. Read the User Agreement and Privacy Policy. Click Submit

Hot tip

Choose a memorable username and one which marks you out as respectable to encourage people to buy from you.

Create an eBay listing

So you have rummaged through your home and you now have a pile of unwanted items you want to sell. To make as much money from them as possible, you have to create a listing. It is the most important part of the selling process: get it right and you will maximise your revenue.

Start an eBay listing

1 Click Sell at the top of the screen and select Sell an item

2 Type in a keyword related to your product

3 Quick sell or Advanced sell? If you want to make your listing stand out, you will want to put in some extra graft so let's go with Advanced

4 On the next page, search for the category which best fits your item. Select the Browse categories tab if the suggested categories are not correct. Click continue

5 If you have a recognized item, eBay will show you many suggested examples of that item. Select the one that is identical to your product

Refining your listing

In order to stand out, you need to ensure your listing draws people to what you have to sell.

1 The title is the first thing people will see:
- Make sure it is spelt correctly. This will not only help when people search but you will sound trustworthy too
- Abbreviate but not too much. Try BNWT for brand new with tags, for example, or BN for brand new
- Above all, make it descriptive. Ensure it gives as much information about the product as possible

2 Be honest when writing your description. Point out any damages. Don't pretend something is rare if it isn't. And explain why you are selling an item. The more you engage with your buyer, the easier your sale will be

3 Check out other people's listings. See how they are describing their items, particularly so if they are selling the same item as the one you are listing

4 Use the Advanced Search option to look at completed listings and the prices they sell for. They are great guides

Hot tip

If you want to see a good list of abbreviations, go to this great guide on the eBay website: bit.ly/P9zZHd

Setting a time scale

When selling items on eBay, you have a choice of timescale. The one you choose depends on how urgent you need to sell and whether you want to maximise your revenue.

How many days?

With eBay, you have a choice of listing an item for one, three, five, seven or 10 days. The crucial thing to remember is that your listing will move up the list as the days go by and it is likely to only be prominent as the duration comes to an end.

1 Most people are said to use eBay on a Sunday evening so if you coincide your listing to end at that point, you will catch the largest number of potential buyers

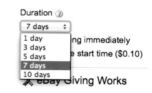

2 To maximise a listing's exposure by ending it at the optimum time, perhaps list on a Thursday evening for 10 days. This will ensure it ends on a Sunday evening and you will also get an extra weekend of exposure for your item

3 If you cannot wait for a weekend to arrive, try and end the listing on a week day evening. More people are found to bid and buy on eBay in the evening than earlier or later in the day

4 Yet if your item is a common one and there are many similar listings, choose an irregular end time (i.e. not an evening) to help to cut down on the competition

Using photographs on eBay

According to eBay, items which carry a photograph are 14% more likely to sell. That sounds like a conservative figure to us. A photograph is one of the most vital aspects of your listing and you want to be able to give your buyer a good look at what you are selling.

Uploading images

1 Within the listing, select the Add function and browse your hard drive for a photograph

2 You will be able to view the image and make amends

Crop
Rotate
Exposure
Brightness

Don't forget

The eBay listing will tell you how many images you can have for free so make use of your maximum allocation.

Photograph tips

1 Take photographs of your objects against a plain background: clutter around an item takes a buyer's attention away

2 Give your item the maximum light. People want to be able to see clearly what they are buying

3 If there is an imperfection, don't hide it. Zoom in and show it so that your buyer feels more confident

4 Photograph items from a variety of angles

5 Don't reduce your images to fit eBay requirements because they will look small on the screen. Crop instead

6 Use a photo hosting website such as ImageShack to host images and link to them for free within your site. Copy the URL and paste it within this HTML code: <img src="xxx" /> (where xxx is the URL). Then copy and paste that code into your eBay listing and it pulls in your image

Introducing Amazon Marketplace

As well as eBay, you can also sell items on Amazon via its Marketplace. When buyers visit Amazon, they see products which are sold via the online retailer itself as well as any other identical new and used products sold via a third party. It is a popular way to sell unwanted items.

Open an account

1 Go to http://services.amazon.co.uk/services/sell-on-amazon/ for Europe (or amazonservices.com/content/sell-on-amazon.htm/ for America)

2 Choose between one of two accounts:
- Basic – charges per item listed
- Pro – has a monthly fee

3 Make your choice and select Start selling. You will have to register a Pro account if you choose Pro otherwise you can start selling straight away

Selling an item on Amazon Marketplace

Once you have begun to sell your item, Amazon takes you through the process of finding an existing product within its online store.

1 Select the product category from the dropdown menu, choosing from books to films, toys to kitchenware

2 Amazon will show you items which best fit your description in the category you have chosen

3 Select Sell Yours Here next to the item which best matches the item you wish to sell

4 Fill in the form with details of your item, inputting:
- Its condition, from new to various levels of used
- A note on the condition if there is something specific
- The price you wish to sell
- The quantity of the item you have for sale
- The delivery method

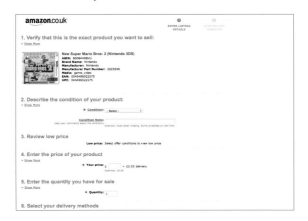

15

5 Review your listing and, if you are happy, then Submit it

Don't forget

Amazon shows you the lowest price at which others are selling your item, which helps when deciding on your own price.

Sell via a free classified advert

There are more traditional ways of selling items online using what are, in effect, classified advert websites such as Gumtree and Craigslist.

As well as items for sale, you can also use them to post items of interest to your community, advertise a job, flat or house or a whole range of services from home building to travel.

Using Gumtree

1 Go to gumtree.com and select Post an ad

2 Choose your region and select a city or county

3 Choose a category and select Continue

4 Fill in the listing form. Many adverts - such as For Sale - are free unless you want it to be urgent or you want to promote it

5 You can add pictures or video to your advert too

Using Craigslist

1 It may not look like much but craigslist.com is packed with free ads and the various regional hubs are well-used

2 Select Post to Classifieds and choose the type of item you are posting, in this case an item For Sale

3 You will be presented with a list of categories so select one that is most relevant to you

4 Input the title, price, location and a description. Bear in mind our eBay description tips for optimum listings

Beware

Craigslist and Gumtree do not have the same level of support as eBay and Amazon Marketplace so take extra care.

Finding postage fees

Don't be left in the dark and undercut yourself when it comes to postage fees. Ensure you quote a buyer the right price every time by going online and checking the exact postage price.

Royal Mail Price Finder

1 If posting from the UK, go to royalmail.com/price-finder

2 Select where your item is going to

3 State the type of item and when you want it delivered to see the price you need to pay. You can buy and print a stamp too

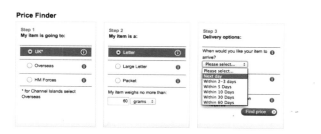

USPS Price Finder

1 Posting from the US? Go to usps.com/ship/service-chart.htm

5 You can ship online or calculate a price for your item

Discover cheap couriers online

Delivery firms are traveling up and down the country every day of the year and they often have spare capacity. It is possible to input your requirements and allow companies with space in their truck to bid on taking your item to the destination of your choice.

Get free quotes

1 Go to uship.com (alternatively, anyvan.com or shiply.com)

2 Chose Get Quotes and select a category

3 Select if the item is being sold via eBay

4 Describe the item and its weight and upload any photos

5 Input the collection and delivery details and set up an account

6 You will begin to get quotes. Simply choose the company you wish to use

Avoiding scammers online

Unfortunately, when you sell items online, you will invariably come across people who attempt to con you out of money or items.

What to watch out for

1. Buyers trying to encourage you to complete a sale outside of the confines of eBay

2. People who insist on having items sent to them before you receive the money, promising they will pay

3. Cheques. If you are paid this way, ensure it clears first before sending an item. Insist on PayPal wherever possible

4. Spoof emails claiming to be from eBay or PayPal. If the email does not contain your name after the word 'Dear' be wary

5. Chargebacks. Some buyers will receive an item, claim there is something wrong or say it has not been received and get a refund from PayPal. Always check a buyers' feedback

2 Buy items for less

Saving money is as good as making money, letting you put more cash in your pocket for future purchases and those extra special treats.

In this section we look at ways of grabbing items for the cheapest possible prices.

Get cashback when you spend

There are two golden rules when buying items online:

- Only buy the items that you need

- Get them for the lowest possible cost

There is no point buying something just because it is in a sale. That is wasting money on items that you do not necessarily need. If you find yourself in that situation, step away from your computer, grab a coffee and go back to your machine later. More often than not, you will decide you do not deperately need that item.

Power up a cashback website

It may surprise you to learn that there are websites which give you cashback just for buying items that you were already planning to buy, from online shops that you use quite often.

Cashback sites give you a set sum of money or a percentage cashback on a vast range of goods ordered via recognized names. You do not get an instant discount: the money owed to you is paid back at a later date, after your purchase has cleared. In each case, the process is the same:

1. Search for the store you wish to buy from

2. See the cashback on offer, click the link and go to the store

3. Buy items in the same way as if you went direct to the site

4. Wait for the cashback to register and then withdraw it once it is made available in your cashback account

Power up a cashback website

There are many good quality cashback websites around. BeFrugal, Ebates, and FatWallet are popular in the US, while great choices in the UK are Quidco and Top Cashback, which also has an American version.

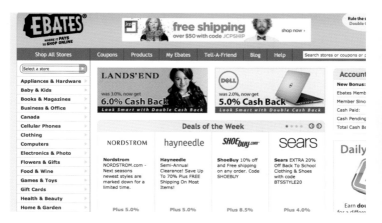

Getting paid

When the retailer pays the websites a commission, the cash will be passed on to you. A section on the websites display any outstanding sums of money as well as the amount sitting in your account, waiting to be withdrawn. Some payments can take a while but be patient.

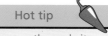

Hot tip

If a promised cashback payment does not appear, the websites allow you to lodge a query whch they will chase on your behalf.

Find and use discount codes

As well as being able to receive cash back on purchases, you can also find online coupons which give you instant money off items.

You will often see a box at the checkout on retail websites which prompts you for a promotional or discount code. Companies like to give regular customers an incentive to return. Offering them free postage and packing or reductions on items is one way they achieve this.

But you do not have to wait for a company to hand you a discount. By going to various websites, you will be able to find promo codes. Often these have been flagged up by the firms themselves but sometimes they are put forward by customers. One thing is certain: if you see a discount code box at checkout, you should instantly start looking for something to fill it with.

Some suggestions
- CouponCodesUSA.com
- Coupons.com
- Myvouchercodes.co.uk
- Hotukdeals.com.
- vouchercodes.co.uk

Type the name of the store into the search engine to list any available discounts. Copy and paste the code into the retailer's promo box.

Hot tip

Type the name of the store you are buying from together with the words 'promo code' in Google to find possible discounts.

Compare prices online

Here is an additional golden rule of buying items online:

- Do not plunge in and buy from the first website you visit

It may well be the cheapest website in the entire world for that particular item but you will not know this for certain unless you compare prices.

Price comparison websites

You can compare prices for a multitude of items whether it be insurance, credit cards, utilities, broadband or individual items. If you can buy it, then there is a good chance you can judge its price against other prices to ensure you are getting the item or service for the lowest cost.

Websites such as comparethemarket.com, moneysupermarket.com, gocompare.com and confused.com in the UK and US sites such as insurance.com and insweb.com are great for comparing insurance products while the likes of Kelkoo, Price Runner, BizRate and Nextag are good for comparing products.

How they work

Insurance and service websites act like a broker and they use the details you input to find you the best deals from a host of individual companies. When using a product comparison service, the websites will search various retail websites and look for the cheapest prices. It is worth using more than one of these services to ensure you capture more of the market, thereby making it more likely you will find a bargain.

Beware

Take into account postage and packing fees when you compare products and check that services are like-for-like.

Buying at the lowest price from Amazon

Amazon is one of the world's most respected and well-used retail websites. It can, however, be quite difficult to find regular promo codes for the site, so often the price you see online is the price you have to pay.

But that should not stop you from hunting out a bargain.

camelcamelcamel

Prices on Amazon often fluctuate up and down so our first tip when using Amazon is to visit the website, camelcamelcamel. This Amazon price tracker shows you the price history of an item and alerts you when the cost of buying it comes down.

1   Find a product you like on the Amazon website

2   Copy the URL of that item

3   Go to camelcamelcamel.com (or .co.uk)

4   Paste the URL into the box which says Enter Amazon URL and click Find Products

5   The website will show you the highest, lowest and average prices for your item and display a graph. Use this to determine whether or not you should wait before buying an item

6   If you wish to wait, fill in the Price Watch box. Input your desired price and email address and click Start Tracking. An email will be sent when the price drops.

Discovering discounted bargains

You can find bargains in every category on Amazon by tweaking the site's URLs. We're going to look at discounts of 75 to 99% here.

1 Click on an Amazon category and make a note of the number at the end of the URL which comes after the code, &node=

2 Type one of the following URLs into your browser:
- amazon.com/gp/search?node=XX&pct-off=75-99
- amazon.co.uk/gp/search/?node=XX&pct-off=75-99

3 Replace the XX with the number from step 1 and press Enter. You will now see lots of discounts. Alter 75-99 if you wish to different numbers to see other price discount ranges

Hot tip

If you want fast, free shipping as opposed to slower free delivery, then consider the paid-for Amazon Prime option.

Take advantage of misspellings on eBay

Some people make mistakes when they are typing. It's a fact of life but one which you, as a savvy shopper, can take advantage of when buying items on eBay.

There are websites which allow you to type in the correct spellings of an item and search for goods which contain a misspelt version of that word.

The idea is that when people type in the names of an item in eBay, they will only be seeing correctly spelt listings. You, however, will now be seeing those poorly spelt ones which very few others will be spotting.

Great websites to try

- Goofbay.com
- Fatfingers.com
- Typozay.co.uk

Each of these allows you to search eBay sites across the world.

To use each one, type in a correctly spelt search term and let the website do the hard work for you. It is also worth typing misspelt words directly into eBay just in case.

Find closing eBay items with no bids

Over the years, eBay has been inundated with Buy It Now items and there are many sizeable companies selling items on the website.

But the auctions still provide a lot of fun and it is possible to grab a wonderful bargain by securing items which are about to end with nobody having bid on them.

Using Last Chance Bid

The website lastchancebid.com is a great way to find those closing eBay auctions with no bids.

1. Go to lastchancebid.com

2. Use the dropdown menu to find the eBay region you wish to use from the many on offer

3. Select the time scale. So, for instance, five minutes means the listing is set to close in the next five minutes

4. Enter a maximum search price or leave it blank if you wish to see everything on offer

5. Choose the category you wish to browse and tap Search

Don't forget

You can use an eBay sniping tool to bid seconds before an auction closes so you can avoid being outbid.

Use Twitter and Facebook

You may use Twitter and Facebook to socialize with friends and to enjoy lively conversations but you can also use these services to save money.

By following or liking companies, you will, in effect, be allowing them to send you adverts via social media. But a lot of companies also offer discounts in this way, giving you promotional codes and notifying you of special offers. Some offer gifts for liking a Facebook page.

Dedicated money saving Twitter feeds

- @retailmenot (USA)
- @momswhosave (USA)
- @fatwallet (USA)
- @moneysavingexp (UK)

There are many more money saving tweeters so it's worth scouring the web for the best, especially if you are interested in certain types of items such as videogames or fashion.

Engage and encourage your friends

Why not share the bargains you find on Twitter and Facebook with your friends? Not only will you be helping them to save some money but they may have spotted an equally good bargain or seen the item you have posted for a cheaper price. It pays to be social.

Don't forget

Only follow the companies you are likely to buy from the most otherwise you may be bombarded with adverts.

Ask shops to match online prices

You can save money on the high street by being savvy online.

How? By going into a store armed with a print out of an item you have spotted online displaying a cheaper price.

Not all stores will match an online price but it is always worth a try.

Use your apps
The good thing about owning a smartphone is that you have the best money saving tool on the planet right in your pocket. Download a barcode-reading app such as Red Laser and you can scan the barcodes of items in stores and discover if you find them cheaper online. Why not show the screen to the store manager and see if he or she can beat it?

Online price matching
Some stores will outline their price match policy. Use the internet to find details of it. John Lewis in the UK, for example, will only price match items that are available on the high street but you can still use the internet to find the best prices on the high street. The John Lewis website will even allow you to submit a price match request online (http://www.johnlewis.com/help/nkupricematchform.aspx).

Using browser add-ons

Instead of visiting individual websites such as eBay or price comparison and voucher services, it is possible to download extensions for your web browser which offer the same functionality.

You could, for example, download an extension for eBay which monitors your buying and selling activity or download an add-on which finds you the best price for a product you are considering buying. Extensions work from within the browser so you do not have to open up a fresh page.

Firefox

1. Go to https://addons.mozilla.org/firefox/extensions/shopping/ for lots of money-saving, shopping extensions

2. Browse the website for the extensions which specifically interest you

3. Click on the extension for more information

4. Select Add to Firefox to download the extension

Hot tip

InvisibleHand is a brilliant Firefox and Chrome extension. It searches for the lowest prices and alerts you to them.

5 Firefox may ask you to confirm the installation

6 Your extension will be available when you restart the browser

Chrome

1 Go to https://chrome.google.com/webstore/category/ext/12-shopping

2 You will see a host of shopping extensions so click the one you like and select Add to Chrome

3 Confirm and it will be added to your Chrome browser

Internet Explorer

1 Go to http://www.iegallery.com/ Addons. Find a shopping add-on and click Add to Internet Explorer

2 Click Add in the pop-up window and it will be installed

Hot tip

Try Ookong on Firefox and Chome to price check the history of items which are available for sale on Amazon.

Find free and cheap apps

There are many free and inexpensive apps available on smartphones but there are ways of ensuring you are always alert to the best bargains.

Using Freeappaday.com

The freeappaday.com website showcases paid-for apps which have been made available for free download. Some developers allow their apps to be temporarily obtained for free to help promote them and generate word-of-mouth publicity. This website will ensure you can pick up some great limited-time freebies.

Price drops on App Store

See when apps are falling in price by keeping a regular eye on 148apps (148apps.com/price-drops/). This looks at Apple App Store prices for both iPhone and iPad. AppShopper (appshopper.com/prices) also allows you to view iOS app price drops.

Cheaper Android apps

AppBrain (appbrain.com/apps/hot/ price-drop/) has an up-to-date list of reduced price Android apps. It also informs you if an app is new or updated.

Don't forget

Why not download the AppBrain app for Android or the App Price Drops by Apple Sliced for iOS to see the latest price falls?

Using a group buying service

By grouping together with other people, you can grab some great bargains. Group buying websites have enticing offers which are available only when a set number of people decide to buy. These are clearly displayed on the websites, together with the time limit.

There are many websites offering group buying offers. The most popular include:

- Groupon

- LivingSocial

- Google Offers

A Typical Deal

Description of offer

Amount to pay

Saving

Time remaining

Number of purchasers

The small print

1 Go to the group buying website of your choice

2 Click Buy Now on a deal you like

3 Input your payment details and your address if you are new to the site

4 Wait until the offer expires and the required number of buyers has been met

5 Read the email you will receive for details of how to redeem your offer

Beware

Only buy items that you actually want and check the terms and conditions. It is very easy to get carried away.

3 Eat cheaply

Whether you want to enjoy a romantic meal for two or save some money on your weekly shopping bill, you'll have enough spare change for some extra special tasty treats after reading this section.

Don't let restaurants eat your money

One of the most pleasurable experiences for many people is eating out.
You get to eat great food without worrying about the preparation or
the washing up. But it is not always stress free: the costs can be rather
expensive so let us look at ways of reducing them.

Pay for discounted gift vouchers

Restaurant.com allows you to grab cut price gift certificates which you
pay for in advance. Do check the terms and conditions relating to each
restaurant before you buy, however.

1 Go to restaurant.com and enter your postcode or select a
popular city

2 Narrow down your search to a specific area

3 Find a restaurant which you like the look of and choose a
certificate before selecting Add To Cart

4 Either Proceed to Checkout to pay for the certificate or continue shopping

Find free discount vouchers

There are websites which offer printable coupons, ranging from two-for-one offers to percentage discounts.

- Concentrating primarily on the big chain restaurants, you can't go wrong at vouchercodes.co.uk/restaurant-vouchers.html

- With pubs, carveries and some independent restaurants, be sure to bookmark myvouchercodes.co.uk/printable-restaurant-vouchers

- There are some takeaway coupons among the chains at moneysupermarket.com/vouchers/supercategory/local-restaurants/30/1/

- An excellent round-up of food outlets in alphabetical order can be found at printable-coupons.blogspot.co.uk/2005/10/restaurant-coupons.htm

Hot tip

Always use a search engine to look for your favourite restaurant, some of which may list special deals such as Early Bird menus.

...cont'd

Use your phone

You don't always need to print out a voucher. Some websites such as stradaoffers.co.uk and pizzaexpress.com/latest-offers give you discount codes on your smartphone. There are also apps available such as Vouchercloud, Capital Eats and Square Meal Restaurants and Bars which show you the latest offers in your location.

Usually these entail:

● Allowing your phone to locate your position

● Showing you restaurants in your area which are offering discounts

● Letting you apply for a code which you can show your server

Children eat for free

If you have children, you'll usually find discounted food for kids in a lot of restaurants.

There are some, however, which will allow your children to eat for free. Try dealseekingmom.com/kids-eat-free/ or type 'kids eat free' into a search engine for any coupons that may be available.

Don't forget

You can also get great deals on restaurants via group buying websites. Again, check the terms and conditions carefully.

Make last minute cheap reservations

By booking online, you can view special offers and compare different restaurants in the area of your choice.

1 Go to toptable.com in the UK or opentable.com in America

2 Select your area

3 On toptable.com, view the entries under the Special Offers tab or on opentable.com, click the Dining Check logo for deals, news and tips

4 Click the restaurant you wish to book

5 Complete the booking form with the date, time and number of people and, if the time and day is available, you can go ahead and book

6 If the time and day is available, you can go ahead and book

Hot tip

Get dining and theatre packages at lastminute.com and pay a visit to the Eat Out For Less section at 5pm.co.uk.

Order takeouts & find discounts

For the times when you want to curl up with a movie and some inexpensive cuisine, a takeout is the perfect solution.

- 5pm.co.uk/takeaway/ has 10 per cent of your first order and discounts at many other takeaways

- JustEat.co.uk has special offers at thousands of takeaways

- Hungryhouse.co.uk also has discounts which show up in the search results for a location

- Grubhub.com has a scheme called Yummy Rummy which you can enter to win discounts and free food and drink once you have ordered three times via the site

Hot tip

Check out the delivery costs. Some takeouts have free delivery if your order is over a certain amount.

Save money on your groceries

There are many ways you can save money on your weekly shopping using the internet to find coupons and to order direct for home delivery.

Using a supermarket comparison website

1 Go to Mysupermarket. co.uk and choose between Groceries, Health & Beauty and Wines

2 Click Start Shopping

3 Fill in your Postcode, name, email and password and click Register

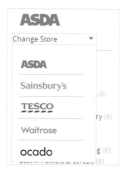

4 Choose a store from the dropdown menu

5 Select an item category from the icons at the top of the screen

Don't forget

As well as groceries, you can also compare health and beauty products as well as wine.

6   Find the items you want by clicking Add to basket beneath each one

Warburtons Thick Sliced Soft White Farmhouse (800g)

£1.20
(15p/100g)

ADD to basket

Cravendale Fresh Filtered Semi Skimmed Milk (2L)

£1.68 any 2 FOR £3.00
(8.4p/7.5p/100ml)

ADD to basket

McCain Home Chips Crinkle Cut (1Kg)

£1.75
(17.5p/100g)

ADD to basket

7   On the right of the screen, you will see how much your basket will cost at the different supermarkets

£3.62
View Basket >

ASDA	£3.62
Sainsbury's	£3.68
TESCO	£3.79
Waitrose	£3.79
ocado	£5.38

CHECKOUT
from ASDA >

8   You can then choose to go straight to the supermarket of your choice to arrange for your delivery

9   In order to check out and create your order with a supermarket, you will need to have an account with that supermarket. These, however, can be created from within the MySupermarket.co.uk website

Finding cheap groceries

As well as being able to price compare, you can also find specific discounts on a whole range of products.

- GroceryGuide.com shows you lots of special offers on groceries for specific stores

- Couponmom.com has printable coupons and grocery deals by state with hundreds of great deals

- Beforeishop.co.uk has lots of discounts and free items and you can see how much all of the offers together will save you each day

- The Shop Scan Save app from Google Play or the App Store uses the UK PayPoint system. Select items and have the app's barcode scanned by the cashier to receive your discounts

Don't forget

By visiting the websites or Facebook pages of products you enjoy, you may stumble upon a useful coupon.

Find free recipes

There are loads of delicious free recipes available to browse and try online, saving you money on cookery books.

- Epicurious.com lets you browse thousands of recipes each of which can be stored in an online account to build up a permanent list of your favourite dishes

- Gojee.com's recipes are as lip-smacking as they look and simply browsing this wonderful-looking website is enough to work up a ravenous hunger

- Punchfork.com has lots of tasty-sounding recipes pulled from various food-related websites, presenting them in a way that makes locating a dish very easy

- BBC.co.uk/food/recipes/ is a great resource that lets you select a dish according to its type, from chicken to chocolate, strawberry to steak

Finding recipes by ingredient

These websites let you input ingredients to find dishes that match.

- supercook.com

- recipekey.com

- recipematcher.com

4 Sort out your home

Doing work around the home can be an expensive business so it is always wise to look for the best ways to cut your costs.

We look at how you can find cost-efficient and reputable tradesmen, rent items and do jobs yourself.

Search for a worker

Finding a tradesman to carry out work on your home can be stressful. Unless you have a recommendation, then you may worry about the quality of work or the reputation of the person doing it. You may also worry about the cost.

Thankfully, there are websites which allow you search for a worker in your area, set your budget, receive quotes and read recommendations.

Using RatedPeople.com

1. Visit ratedpeople.com

2. Click Find a tradesman

3. Select a tradesman description

4. Select the type of job and describe the work you need doing

5. On the next page, you can ask for a quote and also receive advice on the expected cost. Select your budget

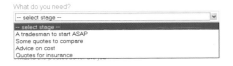

6. Submit the form and receive your information. You can read feedback about the tradesmen who contact you and leave your own comments

Using Workbidder.com

Another great, similar website is workbidder.com which operates in countries across the world including the US, UK, Canada, Australia and New Zealand.

1. Visit workbidder.com and select your country from the flags in the top right-hand corner

2. Select Find Tradesman in the top menu bar

3. Fill in the details of your project, taking care to be as descriptive as you can possibly be, and then tell the site the type of service you want to be provided with

4. The website matches you to suitable companies and tradesmen who will contact you with a quote. You can compare and decide whether or not to accept them

5. You can view ratings to ensure you don't waste money and time on bad tradesman

Hot tip

Need an estimated cost of a job? Visit buildingsheriff.com/tradesmens-day-rates.html for a rough estimate.

Do it yourself : get free DIY guides

There are lots of great guides online to show you how to carry out many essential DIY repairs to improve your home.

- RatedPeople has guides for anything from bricklaying to security (http://www.ratedpeople.com/m/advice/diy-guide.html)

- Hundreds of guides are also available at http://www.diyfixit.co.uk/

- Videos are a good way to show you how to carry out a job and you'll find dozens of them at http://www.diynetwork.com/video-library/videos/index.html

Why not post your work at doityourself.com and use the helpful forum?

Use a paint calculator

While many stores will allow you to return unused pots of paint, the expense and hassle is a pain. So work out the exact amount beforehand.

1. Go to bbc.co.uk/homes/diy/paintcalculator.shtm

2. Input your room measurements (if you do not work in metres, use the built-in imperial to metric converter)

3. Select the type of paint and number of coats needed

4. The website will tell you how much paint you need and how much it will cost in UK pounds

Getting home and car insurance

Price comparison websites are well-known tools to help you compare large numbers of quotes from insurance companies.

By following the instructions on such websites (type 'insurance price comparison' into a search engine to see lots of them), you will be presented with a list of quotes from which to choose, starting from the cheapest prices.

- Always check the insurance quotes are like-for-like

- Use more than one price comparison website

- Play around with the excess and extras, removing and reducing them to see the effect they have on your quotes

- If looking for car insurance, see the effect of adding a second driver

- Try going direct to an insurance company and be aware that some firms are not part of price comparison websites

- Check an insurance company on a cashback website – if they are listed you may save even more cash

- Look on voucher code websites in case an insurance company is running a special promotion

Beware

Never accept a renewal quote on car or home insurance without first checking prices on the internet.

Save money by renting items online

If you need an item for a short period of time, it can make sense to rent it rather than buy. Try rental websites which let you hire items from individuals and businesses.

1 Go to Zilok.com and click the House tab

2 Type in a search term and enter your location

3 When you click Search you will be presented with any items in your area

4 Click Book Now next to the item you want

Rent out your item and make money

Of course you can also rent your own items. Listing them is easy. On Zilok, input the item you want to post in the box to the right of the screen, click OK and fill in the form, registering if you haven't already.

● Why not also try listing your items at rentmyitems.com?

● Listings are free and the site does not charge commission

Don't forget

You can make your rentals more secure by paying using PayPal which prevents anyone from accessing your payment details.

Find or offer storage space online

If you need low cost storage space or if you have an area of your home that you would like to rent out for others to store their items, then you could try.

- Sharemystorage.com
- Storemates.co.uk

1. Register on one of the sites for free

2. Search for storage space depending on size and location

3. Contact the storage owner

4. Confirm the price and space and use the available storage agreement offered by the site

Beware

If you are renting out storage space, make sure you are aware of what is being stored so that you do not fall foul of the law.

Rent out your parking space

For those who live in an area where people pay good money to park, you could make cash by allowing people to park on your property. There are websites which allow others to use your home's parking space.

It is a great way to save money too since the majority of people offer drivers low-cost parking when compared to nearby car parks.

Good websites to try

Each of these websites will allow you to rent somebody else's parking space and also rent out your own.

Check out each one to find the site which best suits you.

- parkatmyhouse.com
- parkonmydrive.com
- parklet.co.uk
- yourparkingspace.com
- p24r.com
- parkingspotter.com
- parkwhiz.com

Don't forget

The websites will take a cut from your parking deal so factor this in when setting a price for your parking space.

5   **Travel on the cheap**

In most cases, the journey matters little – it is the destination that is most important.

Instead of wasting money on getting to places, use the internet to surf for the best deals on planes, trains and automobiles and have cash to spend when you arrive.

Find the cheapest trains

When travelling by train, you definitely need to be on the right track and the one thing to bear in mind is:

- Whenever possible, don't wait until you get to the train station to book your ticket

Booking online will save you having to queue. Most importantly you will save money too.

1. Book as far ahead as you can because that is when you will find the best fares

2. Even if you have to go that day, still go online to book because chances are you will find a fare cheaper than if you buy at a ticket booth

3. Cheap fares can be found by going to sites such as nationalrail.co.uk/times_fares/promotions/toc_index.html and amtrak.com/latest-promotions

4 Avoid postage fees by either picking your tickets up from the station or using sites such as redspottedhanky.com, takethetrain.co.uk and thetrainline.com which don't charge

5 Bear in mind that some websites (including thetrainline.com) have booking and credit card fees. Debit cards and trying different sites can save you money

6 Play around by booking single journeys and even splitting trips if you don't mind changing stations mid-journey

7 Sign up for email newsletters on train service provider websites to be sent promotions and deals

Hot tip

Has a journey on London's Tube delayed you for 15 min or more? You may be refunded: tfl.gov.uk/tfl/tickets/refunds/tuberefund/

Use coaches and buses for less

Often the cheapest modes of public transport are buses and coaches. Try these websites to find some great deals.

Using Megabus

One of the cheapest coach providers is Megabus which runs services across Europe, America and Canada.

1 Go to megabus.com

2 Choose your country

3 In the search and buy window, fill in the details of your journey and tap in your passenger numbers

4 You will see the available trips. Select the one you want and book your journey

Search & Buy

View schedules and buy seats. Select number of passengers, travel locations and dates below:

Number of Passengers	0
No. Concessions	0
No. NUS Extra Cardholders	0
Leaving from	Select
Travelling to	
Travelling by	
Outbound date	
Return date	
Promotion Code?	

Search

▸ Manage Reservations

But the beauty of the web is being able to shop around so also try:

- greyhound.com/en/dealsanddiscounts/default.aspx

- nationalexpress.com/coach/offers/index.aspx

Hot tip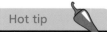

Look out for price comparison websites (try getmeacoach.com) for many other providers at the cheapest possible costs.

Get cheap airline transfers

Use a comparison website to find a low cost way to get from an airport to a city or resort.

- airporttransfers.co.uk

- travelsupermarket.com/c/extras/airport-transfers

- compareairporttransfers.co.uk

- rideflyreservations.com

You should also check the airport websites for your start and end points to discover the best public transport options. These can usually be the most low-cost of all.

Discover a wealth of travel information

Before you embark on a major journey by train or ferry, you could do a lot worse than consult The Man in Seat Sixty-One, a website which provides lots of first class information, saving you time, money and much potential hassle.

Although the website looks rather cluttered, it will prove invaluable, especially if you are set to travel the world.

1 Sit down with a cup of tea: you're going to spend a bit of time researching your journey

2 Start with the homepage at seat61.com

3 Make a choice between travel in the UK & Ireland, Europe or worldwide

4 You can also choose a country via the left hand menu

5 The top menu bar of the website shows you the best places to buy train and ferry tickets

Share your car with others

Fuel prices strike fear into the heart of motorists and yet many of us will drive our cars alone. To save money, consider sharing your journey with somebody else.

Liftshare.com is a great website which allows you to offer your car or look for someone in a position to give you a ride.

1   Click Join for FREE at Liftshare.com

2   Fill in your name, email, country, year of birth and gender

3   Upload a photo which will make you more approachable to others

...cont'd

4 Tell the website where you want to go from and where you are heading as well as how often you make the journey and the times you will do so

5 You need to tell the website what you need: whether it's wanting or offering a lift or even having someone to walk or cycle with

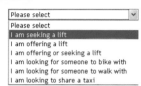

6 Click Find matches to see who can fulfil your request

7 Click Find out more on a match and you can see extra details about them. You use the Contact button to send them an email and begin to set up the lift

Hot tip

You can use liftshare.com to request sharing a taxi which will help to slash any expensive cab fares.

Discover the cheapest fuel

You can ensure that the fuel you fill your vehicle with is the cheapest.

1 Go to petrolprices.com (or why not try gasbuddy.com in Canada and the USA?)

Find the lowest UK petrol price in your area!
10,903 petrol stations and 8,000 daily updates

Enter a postcode or town

[Search]

2 Tap your postcode/zipcode into the box

3 To see the results for petrolprices.com, you need to register for the site

4 The results show you the price, the distance from your location and when it was last updated

Name	Distance	Price	Last Update
A Asda Bolton Blackburn Road, Astley Bridge, Bolton, Lancashire, BL1 8QG	0.94 miles	129.7p	Aug 8th
S Sainsburys Bolton Trinity Street, Bolton, Lancashire, BL3 6DH	1.06 miles	129.9p	Aug 8th
⊙ Bolton Express Bradford Street, Bolton, Lancashire, BL2 1JR	1.04 miles	130.9p	Aug 7th
M Morrisons Bolton Atlas Morningdon Road, Bolton, Lancashire, BL1 4EE	2.02 miles	130.9p	Aug 8th
M Morrisons Harwood Lea Gate, Harwood, Bolton, Lancashire, BL2 3HN	2.36 miles	130.9p	Aug 8th

Don't forget

You can also use the petrolprices.com and gassbuddy.com apps for your smartphone so you can find cheap fuel on the go.

Grab the cheapest flights

Instead of jumping from one website to another, compare the price of flights on a price comparison website such as Skyscanner.net.

1   Click the flag at the top of the screen to select your country

2   In the main Skyscanner box, select where you are going from and to, when you depart and how many people are travelling

3   The website will show you all of the flights going on the days you select and you can select Book

4   To refine your search, select airlines in the left hand menu, select whether you want to go direct or not and alter the times

Use your apps

Signing up to emails from low-cost airlines will inform you of the latest offers. Many have special deals including tax-free flights and the emails will put you in a better position to take advantage.

Don't forget

On the Ryanair website, you can click the dropdown and select No Travel Insurance which is in between Latvia and Lithuania!

6 Save money on holidays

So you've saved up for months for your dream trip and you're ready to book it.

Why not stretch your money a little further with cheaper hotels and less expensive days out, all thanks to the power of the internet?

Get discounts on attractions

You don't have to pay a fortune to enjoy a day out. By using discount websites, you can visit a variety of attractions at a great rate.

1. Try websites such as smartsave.com. Browse the attractions and click to view the terms and conditions. Vouchers can be printed and presented at attractions

2. Visit an attraction's website: some of them, such as Alton Towers, Blackpool Pleasure Beach and Disneyland, offer discounts and special offers for booking direct online

3. Browse themeparktourist.com, a great blog which scours the web for the best deals on theme parks

4. Bookmark websites which are specific to certain countries. For example, in the UK, go to visitbritain.com/en/Cheap-and-free-Britain, daysoutguide.co.uk and moneysavinglondon.com

5. Find attraction discount clubs such as DaysoutUK.com which ask for a subscription fee but offer lots of money off coupons

6. Go to Lonelyplanet.com for some wonderful tips and articles including much advice on free and low cost attractions in cities across the world

Use TripAdvisor to compare prices

Don't get stuck with a costly and awful hotel. Use the reviews on TripAdvisor to discover the best hotels in the price brackets that you can afford and compare lots of different prices from many travel companies at the same time.

1 Go to tripadvisor.com and click the flag in the top right-hand corner to find your country

2 Click the Hotels tab. Type the city name or hotel. Input the check-in and check-out time. Click Find Hotels

3 Refine your search using the left-hand options

4 Select your budget, property type, area and, most importantly, the traveler rating. Work through the refined search results and when you see a hotel you like hover over Show Price

5 Tick the online travel companies from which you would like quotes to see how much your hotel will cost for that duration

Beware

TripAdvisor also has money saving tips for many cities. Search for a city and select Travel Guide.

Find cheap destination guides

You don't have to spend a fortune on a guide book to get the most out of a city.

Great websites

- Travelhoppers.com has many tips to make the most of a destination

- Wikitravel.org is packed with more than 26,000 free destination guides written by travelers

- Inyourpocket.com allows you to view guides as PDFs, iPaper and via an iPhone app

Download Lonely Planet chapters and maps

Why buy an entire guide book when you may only want a certain part of it? Lonelyplanet.com allows you to buy specific chapters of its guide books and you can have the maps for free. The chapters come as PDFs.

Free audio downloads

Rough Guides has free audio downloads available at roughguides.com/website/travel/PhraseBooks/.

Click on the link for Free audio downloads and follow the on-screen instructions.

You can use them on an MP3 player or you can import them into iTunes.

Book cheap hotels online

There are many websites which aim to find you the cheapest hotel deals.

1 Search for promo codes online for the major hotel booking websites. There are many discounts around

2 Use cashback websites and get money back after your booking has been confirmed

3 Go direct to a hotel's website. This can be a cheaper way of booking rather than through a third-party website

4 Try booking each night separately or two at a time if the site won't allow one-day bookings. Some hotel chains work out cheaper if you book this way rather than selecting larger blocks of dates

5 Craigslist.com, Gumtree.co.uk and eBay are three websites where you may well find a hotel giftcard being sold at a discounted price

6 With holiday websites, factor in the price of a flight. Package deals often work out cheaper. Try a few different websites too

Hot tip

Play with the dates. Bookng online lets you be flexible and work out which days will be cheapest.

When the hotel price drops, save money

A service by TripAdvisor called Tingo.com keeps an eye on your hotel booking once you have made a reservation. When the price drops, it makes a note of it, cancelling your original booking, rebooking it and refunding you the difference.

1 Go to Tingo.com. Select the city or hotel you want, fill in the check-in and check-out dates and the number of rooms and people in your party

City/Hotel	Check-in
Paris, France	08/12/2012

2 Look for the large Money Back logo. These are the hotels which Tingo.com will monitor for the lowest prices

3 View the TripAdvisor rating, see the cost and book

4 Tingo sends you emails every time the price drops and a refund will be placed on your credit card within a few days

Hot tip

Spot a cheaper room yourself elsewhere? As long as your room is refundable, just cancel and shift your booking.

Camp in someone's garden

The great outdoors is a great place to be. While campsites are already inexpensive, you may find good deals by camping in somebody's garden.

Join campinmygarden.com for free and you can book a host of garden campsites. You can search by:

- Event
- Location

Simply search for plots by location or event, decide if the price is right and check availability and book.

Offering your garden for camping

Allow people to stay in your garden and generate some cash for yourself. It is free to list your garden.

1. Click Add a new campsite at campinmygarden.com

2. Fill in the location

3. Tick the facilities your 'campsite' has

4. Upload photographs

5. Detail the capacity, currency and price

6. Link your 'campsite' to an event if you wish

Swap your home for a short period

An effective way to cut the cost of your accomodation is to swap your home with somebody else for a short period of time in a location where you would like to enjoy a holiday.

Websites such as homeforexchange.com or homelink.org.uk have been established for this very purpose.

- Such sites command a yearly fee but this eliminates time-wasters and helps ensure only the committed join up

- Swapping your home means you can usually stay for longer without worrying about accommodation costs

- You can live in a residential area and get a real feel for a town or city

- Someone will be staying in your house and will have agreed to look after the property

To swap a home, go to a home swap website and browse houses in the countries or region you would like to stay in, then contact the property owner. People will also be able to view your home. The swaps are formalized via the sites.

Beware

All efforts are made to ensure a smooth home swap but still do your research beforehand before deciding to go ahead

7

Be entertained for less

Whether you are watching television, going to the movies or visiting the theater, you can enjoy it all the more knowing that you have saved some money.

Books, music, film, games... all can be read, listened to, watched and played for less.

Watch movies and TV online

You do not need a costly satellite or cable subscription to enjoy a host of movies and television. Faster broadband speeds mean you can stream great comedies, documentaries, drama and so much more straight to your computer, phone, tablet, games console and even your television.

View movies on YouTube

As well as lots of videos about cats and various homemade productions, YouTube has a great movie channel. Although you have to pay a small sum for some of the films, there are many that you can watch for free.

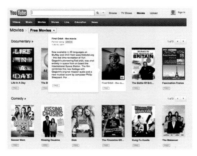

1. Go to youtube.com/movies and click All Categories.

2. Choose the genre you like, including Free

3. If purchasing a movie, you need to sign in using your Google username and password. The money will be taken from your Google wallet

4. Your movie will now be available to watch

Use a movie streaming service

You can save money on movies and television boxsets by taking out a
subscription to a streaming service such as Netflix or LoveFilm.

- Netflix has hundreds of movies and television episodes available each
  month for a set fee

- LoveFilm is a top movie streaming service in the UK that also has
  hundreds of movies available for a set fee

1 Browse films on the Netflix or Lovefilm websites and choose
one. Press play and it will begin to stream

2 Apps are available for both
services on the Xbox 360
(you need Xbox Live Gold)
and PlayStation 3 consoles.
Netflix also steams to the
Nintendo Wii. Simply sign in
via one of these apps

3 LoveFilm can stream to your
iPad and Android device while
Netflix works with Android,
iPhone or iPad

Hot tip

Both Netflix and LoveFilm offer free trial subscription periods so
try before you buy and enjoy some movies for no cost.

There are many more movies at Blinkbox, with lots of them available to watch instantly for free at http://www.blinkbox.com/Movies/Free.

If you are watching from within the United States, try Hulu.com which also has lots of free content although you must view it via a computer.

Independent film and comedy
For those who like to watch diverse, independently made films and shorts, try free-to-view websites such as imovietube.com.

You can also get free comedy at comedycentral.com.

Beware

Streaming movies and television content via the internet can eat into your data package.

Read books cheaply and for free

The best way to save money on brand new physical books is to buy online at retailers such as Amazon.com.

But there are other ways to satisfy your reading habits.

- Sell and buy unwanted physical books

- Join an online book swapping club

- Use an ebook reader and buy cheaper ebooks

- Visit vast online libraries to grab some free books

You should also visit coupon websites (covered in Chapter One) in case they have any discount offers.

Sell and buy unwanted physical books
Amazon Marketplace is a great way to sell your unwanted books.

Underneath Amazon listings are options to buy used books which are cheaper than when purchasing brand new. Any books you sell appear within those listings, making them more likely to be snapped up.

There are other services too including abebooks.com to barnesandnoble.com, both of which offer specific textbook services as well as those which work out a price for your books and make you an offer. Type 'sell books' into a search engine to find many companies of this type.

Hot tip

Sell your books and benefit charities. Greenmetropolis.com offers you a set sum per book sold and it donates money too.

...cont'd

Join an online book swapping club

When you have finished with a physical book, don't just put it back on the shelf. Consider swapping it with somebody else, giving them the pleasure of the book you have read and giving you to chance to enjoy another novel.

1. Go to BookMooch.com

2. To give a book away, click Add which you will find under the Members Home tab and search for the author or book title

3. Click the title of the book you own in the search results and select Inventory Add so others can see you have it

4. For every book you give away to someone who wants your book, you earn points

5. Use those points to search for other people's books and request that they send you a copy.

Use an ebook reader

When buying a Kindle or another ebook reader, you are opening yourself up to thousands of cheaper books. Since they are digitally distributed, you save on printing costs as well as avoiding postage and packing charges.

Many self-publishers distribute their ebooks via the Kindle, iBookstore for iPad, iPhone and iPod Touch and on the internet and while the quality may vary, they can cost you very little.

Grab some free books

Founded as far back as 1971, Project Gutenberg (gutenberg.org) is a wonderful place to pick up more than 30,000 free ebooks.

Each one is out of copyright so it is a perfect website to visit if you are a fan of William Shakespeare or Charles Dickens. There are even audio books available to download.

Google Scholar also has many of these, books, articles from academic journals and peer-reviewed papers which you can view for free if you go to http://scholar.google.co.uk

Don't forget

Amazon Prime users in the US can borrow tens of thousands of books from the Kindle Owners' Lending Library.

Save money at the cinema

Regular cinema goers can save money by finding free preview screenings taking place in their area.

Finding out where these are would be very difficult without the internet and thankfully there are websites which gather this information together in the one place.

Find free movie screenings

- Free Movies UK (fmuk.org.uk)

- See Film First (seefilmfirst.com)

- File Metro (filmmetro.com/)

- Momentum Pictures (momentumpictures.co.uk/)

- Disney Screenings (disneyscreenings.co.uk)

Group buying websites

It is also worth watching out for special deals on group buying websites which sometimes offer cheap cinema tickets.

Get cheap tickets for a show

If you are looking to see a major show or visit the theater, then you will find bargains on the internet. There are many websites offering discounts on tickets and it can be difficult to work out which is the cheapest.

Using a comparison website

1 Go to comparetheatretickets.com for London tickets

2 Input the days you would like to see a show

3 Select the show you would like to watch and click Search

4 The site compares tickets from many different sellers so you can see which one is cheapest

Other notable websites

- Seatchoice (seatchoice.com)

- NYTix (nytix.com)

- Tickets Compared (ticketscompared.com)

It is also worth visiting the website of the theatres. Some of them have last minute tickets available and special offers. Many also have email newsletters which keep you updated with the latest news.

Don't forget

You can apply for tickets to be in the audience for hit TV shows. Try bbc.co.uk/showsandtours/tickets/ or NYTix.com.

Stream music and games

It is possible to stream music and games to your computer, phone or tablet device for free, saving you lots of money.

Using Spotify

Spotify (spotify.com) puts millions of songs at your disposal and you can listen to tunes on a PC, Mac or smartphone.

- The free package allows you to listen to 10 hours of music every month but it contains adverts

- The Unlimited package removes the ads and includes radio while Premium allows you to stream songs to a phone

In order to use Spotify, you will need a Facebook account which you use to sign up.

Playing games via OnLive and Gaikai

The main two services for streaming games online are Sony-owned Gaikai (gaikai.com) and OnLive (onlive.com).

The games themselves are stored in the cloud on remote servers. It means you do not need a cutting edge system in order to play them.

There are many cheap games and free demos from which to choose or you can take out a subscription which cuts the costs of buying games.

Don't forget

You can play 30 minutes of any game on OnLive for free without the need for a credit card.

8 Using free software

There is no need to spend vast amounts of money on software for your PC or Mac.

With excellent free alternatives available to download, you can slash the cost of computing.

Introducing open source software

Some people may tell you that you get nothing in this world for free. That, however, is not true when it comes to software for your PC or Mac.

There are loads of programs available which provide free alternatives to popular expensive software.

Much of this is possible thanks to the hard work of kind and talented coders who work on open source apps, typically producing software which can be freely distributed, changed and improved.

Some great free software packages

- AVG Anti-Virus Free (http://free.avg.com/us-en/homepage) is a brilliant, user-friendly virus protection package for Windows

- 7-Zip (http://www.7-zip.org) lets you pack and unpack compressed files such as 7z, TAR and ZIP formats. Don't forget that Apple Macs allow you to open and compress .zip files

- Ccleaner (http://www.piriform.com/ccleaner) is available for Windows and Mac and it lets you clean up your hard drive, removing cookies, temporary files and other unnecessary clutter

- Audacity (http://audacity.sourceforge.net) gives you immense audio editing power, letting you edit and record sound files to listening perfection... at no cost

- Wordpress (http://wordpress.org/) and its five-minute simple install process gives you incredible blogging power and makes updating powerful websites incredibly easy

Use Photoshop alternative GimpShop

Built to rival Photoshop, GimpShop will allow you to create simple drawings, produce complex graphics and work with photographs - and it will not charge you a penny.

Given that Photoshop can cost as much as $699, that's quite some saving. GimpShop works on both Windows PCs and Macs and it can be downloaded from gimpshop.com.

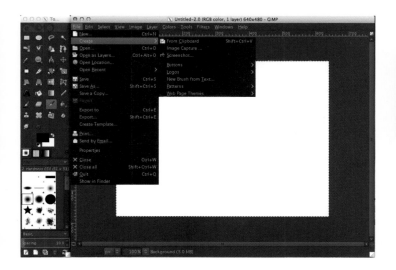

Hot tip

To get the most out of GimpShop, read its comprehensive set of free tutorials at http://gimpshop.com/tutorials.

Find an alternative to Microsoft Office

Why spend a small fortune paying for Microsoft's Office suite when you can download a fully-featured alternative for free? LibreOffice is arguably the best open source office suite around and it provides a:

- Word-processor (Writer)

- Spreadsheet (Calc)

- Presentation app (Impress)

- Graphic editing app (Draw)

- Database (Base)

- Equation editor (Math)

Download LibreOffice

1 Go to http://www.libreoffice.org/download/ and click the option for Main installer

2 Save the file, double click and select Run

3 Follow the install wizard

Opening LibreOffice

1 Double click the LibreOffice icon

2 Choose the application you want from the menu

Using LibreOffice

Most people will use the word processor of LibreOffice the most. Let us look at some of the most useful parts of it.

Open and save icons

Select your fonts

Bold, italics and underline

Spellcheck

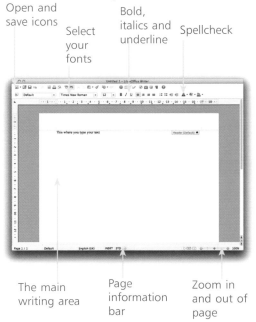

The main writing area

Page information bar

Zoom in and out of page

Hot tip

Click Tools>Customize and select the Keyboard tab to see a list of keyboard shortcuts which will speed up your work.

Free Desktop Publishing packages

Desktop publishing (DTP) has made it easy for people to produce their own printed newsletters and magazines but professional packages such as those by Quark and Adobe are very expensive. Depending on your level of expertise, you may want to consider one of these two packages.

PagePlus Starter Edition

Serif has a strong reputation for producing great software and its long-established PagePlus DTP packages have always been critically well received.

The company has a free version called the PagePlus Starter Edition which you can download by going to http://www.serif.com/desktop-publishing-software/

"An invaluable tool for creating professional publications easily." *

Scribus

If you want a more powerful QuarkXPress or Adobe InDesign alternative, then try the open source package Scribus http://www.scribus.net/canvas/Scribus.

The free package can produce PDFs which are ready to be sent for professional printing. It's not an easy program to understand if you are a novice but it sure is powerful.

Hot tip

If you own an Apple Mac, you can use the inexpensive word processor, Pages, to design simple layouts.

Get free online storage space

Cloud storage is a popular way of backing up and keeping a copy of your files. It also allows you to access them on any internet-enabled computer. There are many such services and each offer a free option.

Dropbox

Dropbox (www.dropbox.com) is an amazing service that can be used for free. You get 2GB of storage as standard but for each friend you recommend, you receive a further 500MB. There are no restrictions on what you can upload to your space.

When you install Dropbox on your computer, it acts like any other folder on your PC or Mac. A small, permanent logo is placed on your desktop. Clicking on it opens your Dropbox folder. You can then move files back and forth just as you would between normal folders.

Apple iCloud

The iCloud service is specially geared towards Apple users. It works on all of Apple's devices - the iPad, iPhone, iPod Touch and the Mac - and it seamlessly syncs a wealth of data, storing it all on remote hard drives, ready to be accessed.

With iOS 5 or iOS 6 installed on your iPhone, iPad or iPod Touch and with OS X Lion or Mountain Lion on your Mac, you are fully equipped to start using iCloud.

It allows you to store your music, movies, photos, apps, books, TV shows, documents, email, contacts, calendar and so much more and for Apple owners it is a great addition.

Using Google Drive and documents

Google Drive is a service which allows you to store files online for free. You also get access to an online office suite which includes a word processor, spreadsheet and presentation package. You can upload and access photographs, videos, documents, PDFs and any work which you create using Google Docs.

Your uploaded files can be accessed via:

- A PC or Mac
- An iPhone or iPad
- An Android phone or tablet

Google Drive allows you to collaborate with other people on projects. Files can be shared and they can also be edited by others. It is a competitive service too. You are given 5GB of storage space for free.

Getting started with Google Drive

1 Go to https://drive.google.com/start on your browser

2 Click on Sign In and input your Google login

3 Click Try Google Drive to get started

Hot tip

You can find out more about the delights of cloud computing with our book Cloud Computing in easy steps.

9 Ensuring talk is cheap

Whether you are selling your mobile phone or avoiding high phone charges, the internet is the friend you need to call upon.

We look at ways of making the most of your talk time.

Using an online mobile phone service

For those living in the UK, the giffgaff network offers a cheaper way of making phone calls. It's an online-only mobile phone service run by the company behind O2.

If you feel comfortable with a service that doesn't offer you telephone support and relies on the community to resolve problems, then this could well be for you.

1. Order a free SIM at giffgaff.com

2. View the phone plans. They range from as little as £10 which will get you 250 minutes of talk time, unlimited internet data and unlimited texts each month

3. There are no contracts so you can operate your account month by month and you will be able to cancel at any time

4. Its per minute prices are less than half those of its UK rivals so if you go over your talk time, you will still be able to talk for less

Hot tip

You can buy gigabags from £5 a month which give you 500MB of mobile data. They are perfect for internet dongles.

Avoid high call charges

Calling 08 numbers in the UK can be very expensive, especially if you are using a mobile phone. Luckily you can find alternative landline numbers which you will be able to call for less or within your inclusive minutes.

1 Go to saynoto0870.com

2 At the top of the page, click Search to find an alternative number

3 Enter a Company Name or enter a 08 phone number and click Search

4 The site will present you with a list of numbers

Main Database					
Company Name	0870 / 0871	0844 / 0845	01 / 02 / 03	Freephone	Other Information
Abbey (Groupo Santander)				0800 670640	Home Insurance Menu. Hold for person & transfer to banking (maybe India - pot luck)
Santander		0845 934 4900	01908 238046		**Card Services - Lost & Stolen** ONLY call Geo using a MOBILE !!
Santander		0845 765 4321	01908 719037		**Card Services** Straight to agent Also for: 0845 972 4724
Santander		0845 972 4724	01908 237963		**Customer Services Menu** ONLY call Geo using a MOBILE !!
Santander		0845 972 4724		0800 1697903	Customer services, Lost & Stolen, etc. Message says for internal use only
Santander		0845 609 0014	01908 238046		**Customer Services Menu** ONLY call Geo using a MOBILE !!

Hot tip

The Say No To 0870 Call Intercept app on Google Play alerts you to any premium numbers and finds a cheaper alternative.

Sell your mobile phone online

Don't let your old cellphone/mobile handset gather dust. Turn it into money by finding the best phone recycling deal online.

Type your mobile phone handset model into a phone comparison website such as:

- mobilephonerecycling.co.uk

- moneysavingexpert.com/phones/mobile-recycling

- compareandrecycle.com

They will give you a list of prices.

Simply choose the recycler you wish to use, send them your handset and receive your money.

Check prices on eBay

Before you agree to sell to a recycler, check out eBay prices first.

1 Go to eBay.com and sign in

2 Select Advanced Search

3 Tick the box for Completed Listings

4 Type your phone model into the search box

5 You will see how much your handset has been selling for on the site

Find Items

Enter keywords or item number

Phone — All words, any order

Exclude words from your search

See general search tips or using advanced search options

In this category:

All Categories

Search

Save this search to My eBay

Search including

Title and description

✓ Completed listings

Price

Show items priced from $ — to $

Buying formats

Auction

Buy It Now

Beware

Some mobile phone recycling companies will reduce the price they pay you if it is slightly damaged. Check the small print.

Make free calls and send free texts

Use your broadband connection to make phone calls and avoid high charges. Using a service such as Skype, you can call other users for free and the service is available on so many different platforms. It is also a very convenient way to keep in touch.

- Make one-to-one video calls
- Call other Skype users
- Use instant messaging
- Share your screen

There are charges for calling phones, forwarding calls or sending a SMS.

1 Go to Skype.com and click Download

2 The Skype app will install on your machine

3 Use a headphone and microphone to make calls and use your webcam for video

Send free text messages via a Mac
With iMessage on Mountain Lion, you can send free text messages via an internet connection to phones around the world.

Instant messaging
An instant messaging program such as Windows Live Messenger or Google Talk allows you to send written and pictorial notes to other users in real time.

10 Be creative & make money

By putting your creative talent to good use and investing your time, you could make a lot of money.

Whether you are producing unique gifts or writing a book, there is no harm in profiting from your talented endeavors.

Sell your own items: Etsy and Folksy

For those who have a talent for creating beautiful items and gifts, the artisan websites Etsy and Folksy are a welcome haven, allowing people to buy and sell an array of weird and wonderful homemade goods.

Selling on Etsy.com

The largest creative website is Etsy.com which claims to have a community of 15 million buyers and creative businesses. It works in a similar fashion to eBay, only the items on sale are tailored more towards fashion, unique crafts, and home and garden items that you will not find on the high street.

1. Go to etsy.com/sell

2. Click Open an Etsy Shop

3. Sign in using your Facebook account or register

4. You'll be asked to specify a country and currency

5. You'll be ask to input a shop name. This can be a temporary one at first while you think of a permanent one

6. Click List an Item to be taken to the listing page

7   Work through the form inputting:

● Who made the item

● The category

● A photo (click the box
and browse your hard
drive for an image)

● An eye-catching title
for the item

● A vivid description
and a shop section

● The recipient, category, occasion and style

● Tags which allow for easier searching

● The materials used and the price, quantity and shipping
information for your item

8   Click Preview Listing and save it as a draft

9   Input your payment methods (e.g. key in an email associated
with your PayPal account)

Don't forget

It costs $0.20 to list an item for up to four months and Etsy
takes a 3.5% fee on the sale price.

...cont'd

Selling on Folksy.com

While Etsy allows you sell across the world, you may only want buyers from the United Kingdom. If that is the case, than Folksy.com is for you.

1　Go to Folksy.com and click Register

2　Decide on a username and password

3　Click Start Selling in the top left-hand corner

4　Decide whether you want a Basic account or pay £30/year for Folksy Plus and avoid listing fees

5　Input your shop name and describe the shop. You then need to upload a banner, give your real name and input your PayPal email address

Don't forget

On a Basic account, it costs £0.15 to list an item for up to four months and Etsy takes a 6% fee + VAT on the selling price.

6 Click Add a listing and fill in the form with your:

- Item title
- Description
- Materials
- Colors
- Photo
- Story of your item
- Quantity, price and posting information

7 Preview your listing and send it live if you like it

Selling an ebook online

They say everyone has a novel in them. For those who have bashed out enough quality words, going down the route of self-publishing can prove to be a great way of making money.

There are two main platforms:

- Print-on-demand
- Ebooks

While we do not have the room to explore these in incredible detail, we will take a look at each in turn.

Print-on-demand

Websites such as Lulu.com and Blurb.com allow you to create a printed book which you can then sell online.

The idea is that you upload your writing to one of the websites, add a cover and decide the format of your book and how much you wish to charge for it, taking into account how much it will cost to print.

When somebody buys your book, the companies will print it on an order-by-order basis.

They will send the book to your buyer and pay you the difference between the price you set and the cost of printing.

The good thing is you do not have to get involved in distribution.

Ebooks

Book readers and tablet computers have opened up the ebook market to the point where millions of digital books are being sold every year.

The most popular platforms for ebooks (and the websites for self-publishing) are:

- Amazon Kindle (kdp.amazon.com/self-publishing/signin)

- Apple iPad (https://itunesconnect.apple.com/WebObjects/ iTunesConnect.woa/wa/bookSignup) books

- Android tablets (support.google.com/books/partner)

Each site explains the process and how much money you can potentially earn. It is also worth bearing in mind that Kindle apps are available for PCs, Macs, tablets and smartphones which greatly widens the audience for your book.

Hot tip

If you own an Apple Mac, then download the free iBooks Author app from the Mac Store

Sell your own artistic designs

If you have a talent for art and design, you can produce a range of
T-shirts, posters, caps and gifts which can then be sold online. Sites
such as cafepress.com, zazzle.com and spreadshirt.com let you upload an
image, place it on a range of products and sell them.

The hard work is in coming up with the design. The websites take care
of the rest. We are going to look at Cafepress.com.

1 To get started, go to http://members2.cafepress.co.uk/CnL/
GetStarted

2 Click Upload an Image

3 Find an image that is at least 600x600 pixels

4 Enter your name, title and description and tag the image for
easy search

5 Save the design and you will then be prompted to set up an
account

6 The website will ask you which products to which you wish to
add your design

Hot tip

When using Cafepress.com, you can even set up your own
shop that can be linked to your website or blog.